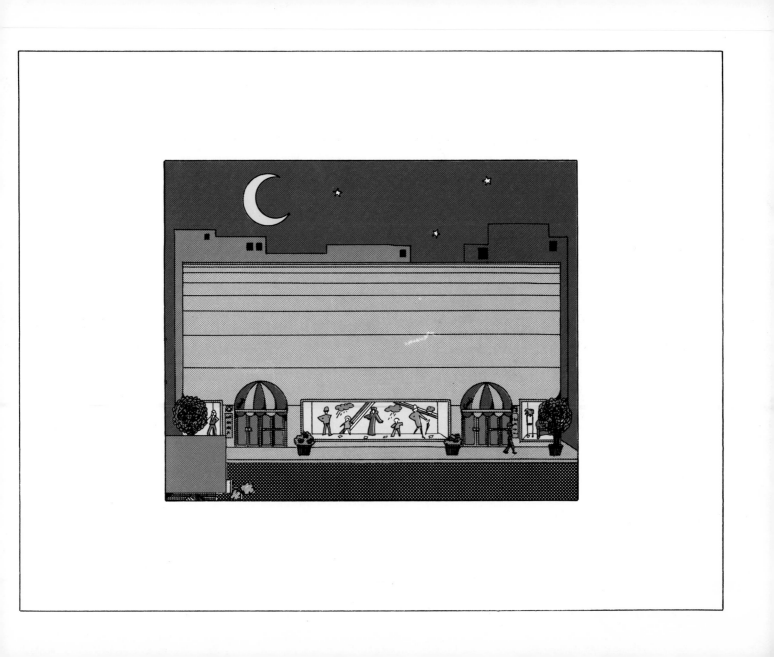

DEPARTMENT STORE

by Gail Gibbons

STORE
HOURS

Monday-
Thursda
Saturd
10-
Friday
10-9

THOMAS Y. CROWELL   NEW YORK

For Becky and Kate

Department Store
Copyright © 1984 by Gail Gibbons
All rights reserved.
Printed in the United States of America.

Library of Congress Cataloging in Publication Data
Gibbons, Gail.
    Department store.
    Summary: Describes the activities in a busy
department store during a typical day.
    1. Department stores—Juvenile literature.
[1. Department stores]   I. Title.
HF5461.G52 1984   381′.1   83-45053
ISBN 0-690-04366-X
ISBN 0-690-04367-8 (lib. bdg)

1 2 3 4 5 6 7 8 9 10
First Edition

Also by Gail Gibbons
New Road!   ·   The Post Office Book   ·   Trucks
Locks & Keys   ·   Clocks and How They Go
illustrated by Gail Gibbons
Cars and How They Go

Special thanks to Richard Brode and Marge Sweet of Gimbels,
New York division, and Thom Chasse and James Goetcheus
of JCPenney Co., Lebanon, N.H.

The shopping day hasn't begun yet, but department store employees are already at work, tidying up from the day before.

At the back of the building, big trucks pull up to
deliver the new merchandise ordered by the store.
Delivery trucks will come and go all day long.

In the store's office, salespeople pick up money for their cash registers, and the forms they will use to keep track of what they sell that day.

When everyone is ready

and the entrance lights come on...

the doors are unlocked and the customers come into the store.

The shopping day begins.

Popular items on the first floor catch their eyes.
The department managers know what will sell quickly
and where to place it.

The customers browse through the aisles.

Some of the shoppers begin to move up and down to the other floors…

and into the separate departments.

They won't have to shop at many different stores to find
what they want....

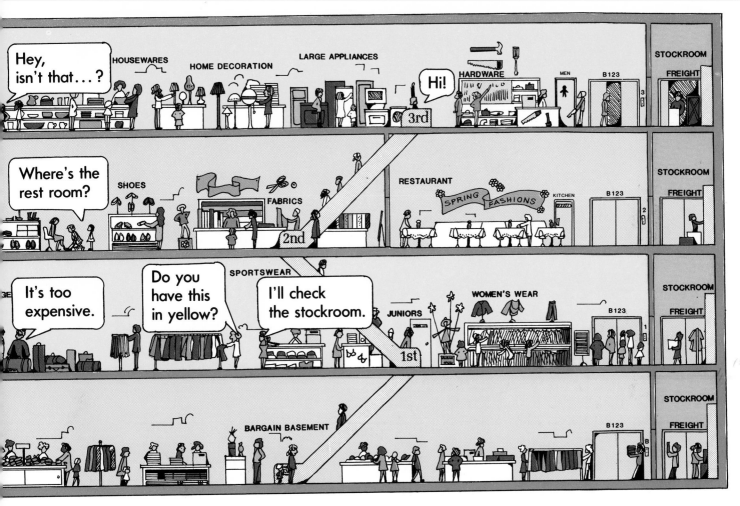

Everything is under one roof!

Down in the stockroom, new items are unpacked...
ticketed...and sent off...

to the correct departments.

Display artists work with the department managers to arrange the merchandise in an exciting way.

Salespeople help customers try things on...

test out equipment...

measure... and find things, too.

A "Special Sale" on bedroom slippers is going on in the
Bargain Basement. Customers come to snatch up good buys.

It's lunchtime. The store has its own restaurant.
While the customers eat, they are entertained by
a fashion show.

Time to shop again.
Some purchases are too big to be carried home…

so the salesperson orders a duplicate from the store's
big warehouse or direct from the factory.
A truck will deliver it to the customer's home.

Many customers pay for their purchases with cash.

Others say, "Charge it."
The store's Credit Department will send them a bill later.

In the department store Showroom, a toy company
representative calls on the store's toy buyer. The buyer
decides what toys he wants to order for the store to sell,
and a delivery date is arranged.

The store has a Customer Service Department and a
Gift Wrap Department, too.

A voice comes over the speaker system...

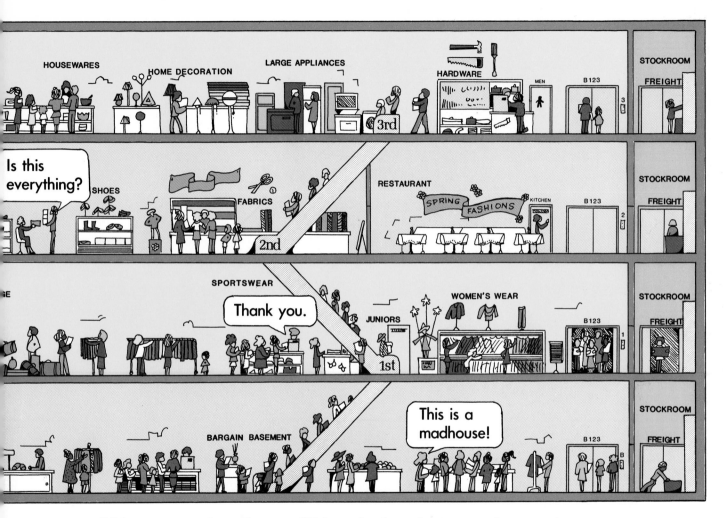

"Shoppers, the store will be closing in ten minutes.
Please take your purchases to the nearest cashier. Thank you."

Guards check to make sure all customers are out of the store. Then the doors are locked.

The cashiers count their money and bring it to the office with their records of the day's business.

The employees go home for the night, the lights are turned off, and the burglar alarm is set.

The shopping day is over at the department store.

1

For thousands of years people traded with each other to get the food, clothing, and other things they needed.

2

Then people began to use money to buy things. They traveled to town marketplaces, where small stalls lined the roadside. Each stall owner had his own special wares to sell.

3

As towns and cities grew in size, the roadside stalls became enclosed stores that sheltered the owners' things from bad weather and kept thieves out. The customers shopped from store to store.

4

Later, in early America, small towns didn't have many shops because there weren't enough customers. Instead, people shopped in one "general store." In the general store you could buy almost anything.

5

As towns became bigger, these stores became bigger, too. They separated their merchandise into different departments. Customers found what they were looking for faster, and they didn't have to go from store to store.

They were shopping in a modern department store.